# A 2025 CALENDAR

## A Tool for ESL Teachers

### CREATED BY:
### LYNN RICHARDSON

# 12

## MONTH ESL/ART
## LEARNING ACTIVITIES

# CONTENTS

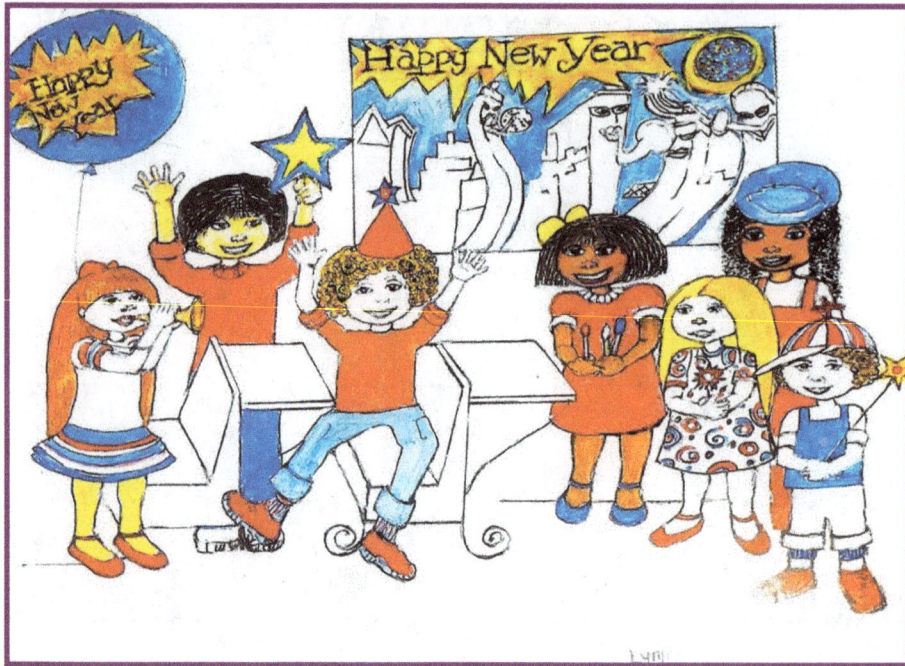

# JANUARY

## CELEBRATING 2025 AROUND THE WORLD

http://www.educationworld.com this website shows how people celebrate New Year around the world. Students can explore and engage in research on how they can celebrate New Year traditions around the world.

This website includes New Year Eve traditions from all around the world. Students could pick one, two, or any country of their choice in order to explore their traditions, write descriptions about them and what they liked about them, and draw their own creative illustrations.

# JANUARY A 2025 CALENDAR

| SUNDAY | MONDAY | TUESDAY | WEDNESDAY | THURSDAY | FRIDAY | SATURDAY |
|--------|--------|---------|-----------|----------|--------|----------|
|  |  |  | 1 | 2 | 3 | 4 |
| 5 | 6 | 7 | 8 | 9 | 10 | 11 |
| 12 | 13 | 14 | 15 | 16 | 17 | 18 |
| 19 | 20 | 21 | 22 | 23 | 24 | 25 |
| 26 | 27 | 28 | 29 | 30 | 31 |  |

7

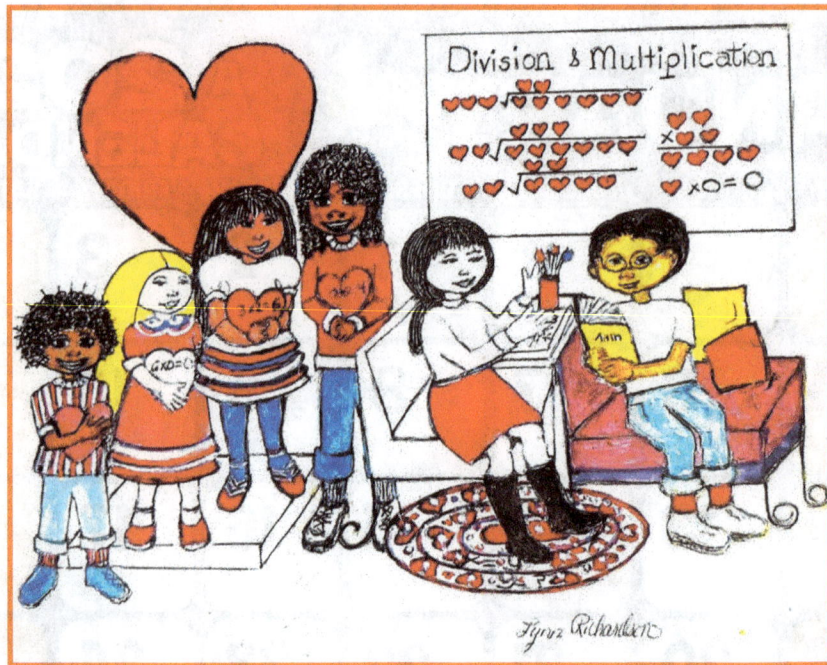

Lynn Richardson

# FEBRUARY

## BLACK HISTORY MONTH

One cannot recognize American history without acknowledging or celebrating the achievements and contributions of black people in America. Black History month has historically been celebrated in America, Canada, and the United Kingdom. Each Black History month originally started out as Black History Week and over time had grown to last and be celebrated for 30 days. Many African Americans celebrate black history throughout the year. https://www.weareteachers.com. This website is a wonderful educational tool which gives the history and offers activities that honor Black History month. During the month of February many schools hold festivals and plays that depict how it all began featuring the lives of pioneers like Frederick Douglas and Harriet Tubman who helped to pave the path and lead the way. Both students and teachers are encouraged to read about, write about, and think about the pioneers who inspired them and how their contributions have affected our lives today. These events and activities have become nationally spread and celebrated throughout the country in community groups, museums, churches, and other groups that honor all the people and their achievements up to the present day.

# FEBRUARY

## A 2025 CALENDAR

| SUNDAY | MONDAY | TUESDAY | WEDNESDAY | THURSDAY | FRIDAY | SATURDAY |
|--------|--------|---------|-----------|----------|--------|----------|
|        |        |         |           |          |        | 1        |
| 2      | 3      | 4       | 5         | 6        | 7      | 10       |
| 9      | 10     | 11      | 12        | 13       | 14     | 15       |
| 16     | 17     | 18      | 19        | 20       | 21     | 22       |
| 23     | 24     | 25      | 26        | 27       | 28     |          |

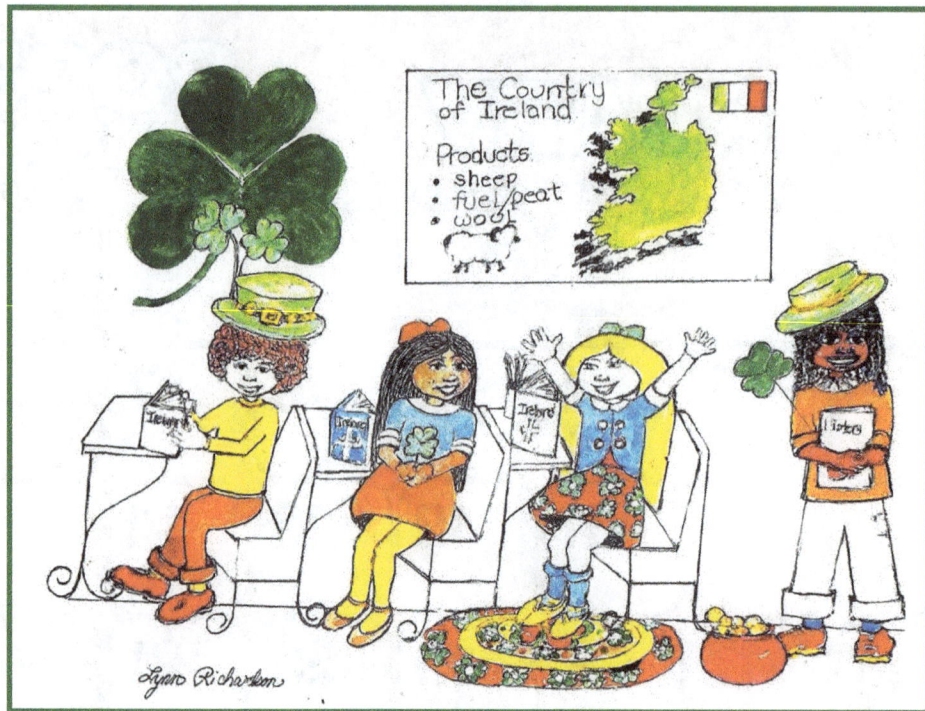

# MARCH

## MARCH THEMES & ACTIVITIES

https://www.clutterfreeclassroom.com is a great website that offers exciting resources for teaching and celebrating holidays and events like Women's History Month, Saint Patrick's Day, and Dr. Suess's birthday. All of these events took place historically during the month of March all each can be celebrated in special ways.

https://www.kidsactivities.net. This website has great activities for March themes and children's learning activities.

When teachers bring their classes to visit the library students can pick the book with the holiday or event of their choice. Then they must read and conduct independent research on any of the three choices of either Women's History Month, Saint Patrick's Day, or Dr. Suess's birthday. Students will engage in writing descriptive paragraphs on the history of each event, on how it got started, and describe what challenged their interest the most. In conclusion students can draw, create, and color their own illustrations as an art activity. As an added art activity for the Saint Patrick's Day holiday, students can celebrate Saint Patrick's Day by creating their own designs by tracing and drawing shamrock patterns which can be cut out and pasted underneath their written paragraphs.

# MARCH

## A 2025 CALENDAR

| SUNDAY | MONDAY | TUESDAY | WEDNESDAY | THURSDAY | FRIDAY | SATURDAY |
|--------|--------|---------|-----------|----------|--------|----------|
|        |        |         |           |          |        | 1 |
| 2 | 3 | 4 | 5 | 6 | 7 | 10 |
| 9 | 10 | 11 | 12 | 13 | 14 | 15 |
| 16 | 17 | 18 | 19 | 20 | 21 | 22 |
| 23 | 24 | 25 | 26 | 27 | 28 | 29 |
| 30 | 31 |   |   |   |   |   |

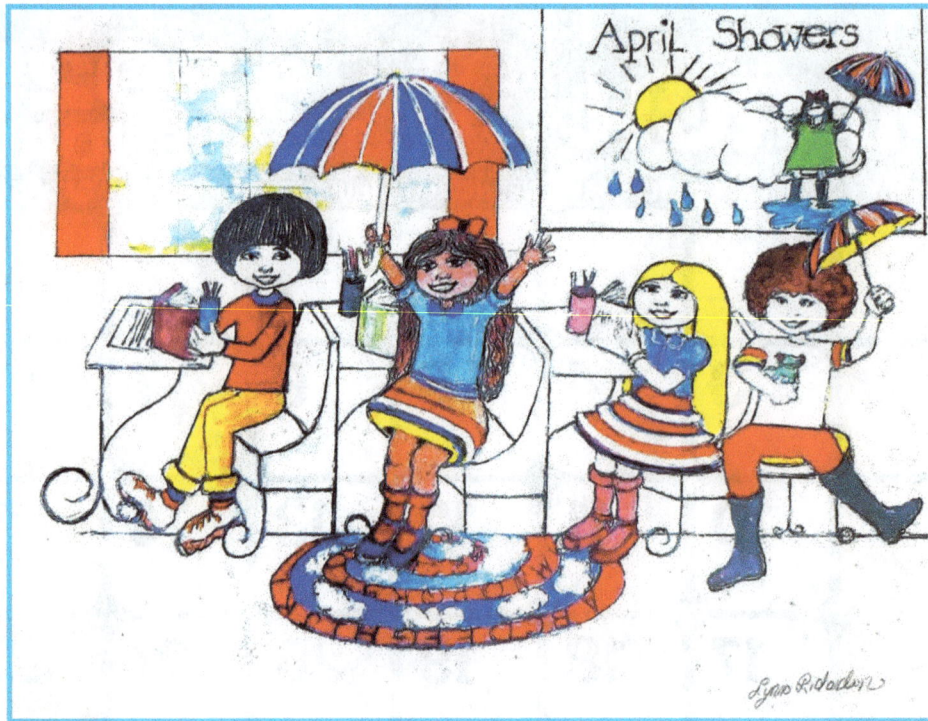

# APRIL

## FAVORITE CLOUD 9

https://www.elementaryschools.science.com is a website which offers a lesson plan entitled Cloud 9. The Cloud 9 lesson plan teaches the students about the different types of clouds, how they are formed, and describes the characteristics of each type of cloud. After the class researches this material, students may choose their favorite cloud, write a short composition about why they chose their favorite cloud, and describe their cloud's characteristics. Following a class discussion, students can either draw, paint, or use cotton balls as an art activity to display their favorite cloud creations. This learning should conclude with the children attaching their creative cloud formations to be put beneath their short written compositions.

# APRIL

## A 2025 CALENDAR

| SUNDAY | MONDAY | TUESDAY | WEDNESDAY | THURSDAY | FRIDAY | SATURDAY |
|--------|--------|---------|-----------|----------|--------|----------|
|        |        | 1       | 2         | 3        | 4      | 5        |
| 6      | 7      | 8       | 9         | 10       | 11     | 12       |
| 13     | 14     | 15      | 16        | 17       | 18     | 19       |
| 20     | 21     | 22      | 23        | 24       | 25     | 26       |
| 27     | 28     | 29      | 30        | 31       |        |          |

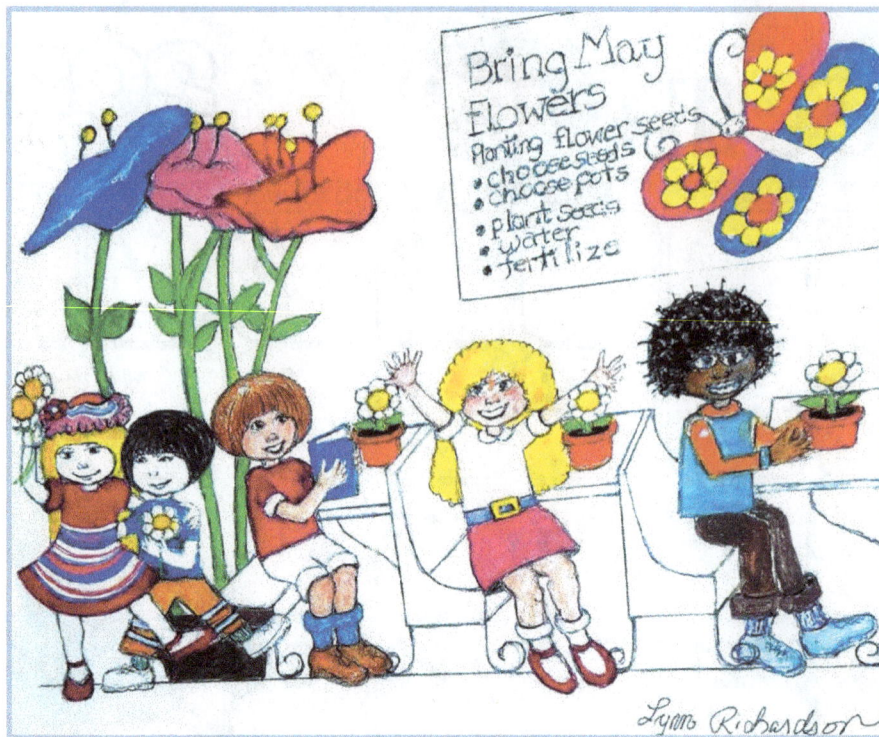

# MAY

## PLANTS & FLOWERS

https://www.weareteachers.com is a website that has compiled a list of classroom gardening ideas, lessons, tips, and tricks that can help teachers help their students learn about plant life, plant cycles, botany, and ecosystems. This site offers printable that display the parts of plants, anchor charts, and videos on plant life cycles. Then the teacher will pass out handouts about information on flowers/plants that should encourage students to draw all the parts of a plant and label each part. A classroom discussion should follow in which students engage in describing the characteristics of each plant or flower. The teacher may have bought several flower or sunflower seeds for each student to plant. The teacher will go ahead and model the seed planting process so that students would know how to plant their seeds properly and water them. Each student should have their own chart of plant growth as they begin to go on their adventure to nurture and water their plant/flower and watch it grow, grow, grow!

# MAY

## A 2025 CALENDAR

| SUNDAY | MONDAY | TUESDAY | WEDNESDAY | THURSDAY | FRIDAY | SATURDAY |
|--------|--------|---------|-----------|----------|--------|----------|
|        |        |         |           | 1        | 2      | 3        |
| 4      | 5      | 6       | 7         | 8        | 9      | 10       |
| 11     | 12     | 13      | 14        | 15       | 16     | 17       |
| 18     | 19     | 20      | 21        | 22       | 23     | 24       |
| 25     | 26     | 27      | 28        | 29       | 30     |          |

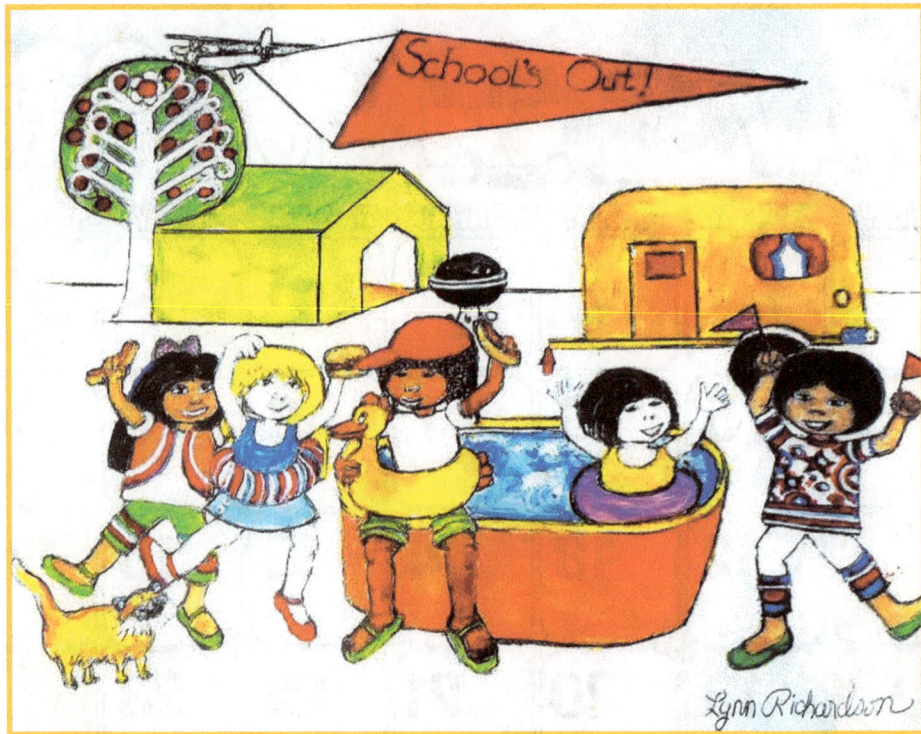

# JUNE

## GRANDMOTHER OF JUNETEENTH

Opal Lee and What It Means To Be Free: The True Story Of Juneteenth by Alice Fay Duncan / illustrated by Ketura A. Bobo. This is a wonderful book for     elementary students to read about the true story of Opal Lee, the Grandmother of Juneteenth. This book should be available at your local school library and available also on Amazon.

https://www.pbs.org is a lesson plan that helps students explore and understand the history and context around the Juneteenth holiday in the United States. Topics in this lesson include the history of racial injustice in the United States, the Civil War, and the limitations of the Emancipation Proclamation. Students will be encouraged to explore the modern significance of Juneteenth and its long term impact. The teacher can adjust the learning activities of this lesson plan accordingly to the appropriate age level.

# JUNE

## A 2025 CALENDAR

| SUNDAY | MONDAY | TUESDAY | WEDNESDAY | THURSDAY | FRIDAY | SATURDAY |
|--------|--------|---------|-----------|----------|--------|----------|
| 1 | 2 | 3 | 4 | 5 | 6 | 7 |
| 8 | 9 | 10 | 11 | 12 | 13 | 14 |
| 15 | 16 | 17 | 18 | 19 | 20 | 21 |
| 22 | 23 | 24 | 25 | 26 | 27 | 28 |
| 29 | 30 | | | | | |

# JULY

## THE RED, WHITE, AND BLUE AMERICAN FLAG

https://www.larryflazo.com website is a fantastic website that provides teachers with resources that can help students learn about the fourth of July.

This website includes a special ESL Fourth of July lesson, a Fourth of July site from the History channel, and two resources https://www.howstuffworks.com that could be modified by teachers to make them more accessible to English Language learners. The teacher will access https://www.theamericanflag.com website are students to explore colors, concepts of freedom, and symbols that represent the meaning of freedom. After the students learn about the concept of freedom and what each color represents, they may write a descriptive sentence about what freedom means to them. Students are challenged to create their own Fourth of July flag or Fourth of July Angel flag and employ the colors of red, white, and blue in the creations of their own designs.

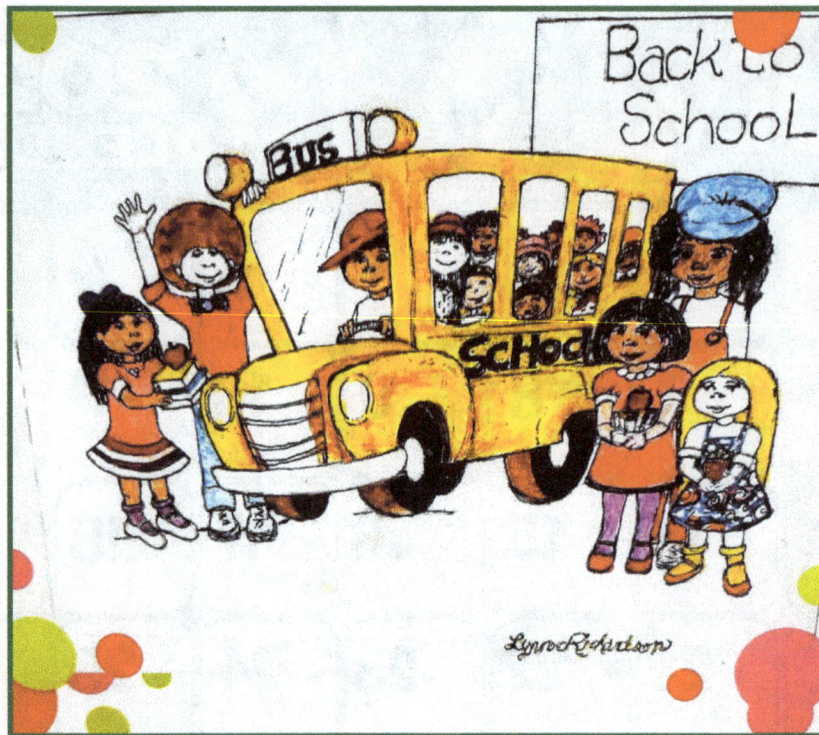

# AUGUST

## BACK TO SCHOOL MAGIC BUS WORKSHEET

https://www.teacherspayteachers.com Teachers Pay Teachers is a website that offers a pack of Magic School Bus Video Worksheets for every episode of the show. Each worksheet contains a single page guide that will keep the students engaged while learning and watching Mrs. Frizzle and her class head out on every exciting field trip.

On the first day of school students will get to design their own "Back to School Magic Bus" worksheet. Pictures of school buses will be handed out so that the students can design and create their own "Back to School Magic Bus" Worksheets. Now the students could record each students' name, address, name of their school, the principal, new teachers, and homerooms, etc. Each student could now record the date that they started back to school and make a list of new friends and old friends that they were glad to see on that day.

# AUGUST

**Back To School**

## A 2025 CALENDAR

| SUNDAY | MONDAY | TUESDAY | WEDNESDAY | THURSDAY | FRIDAY | SATURDAY |
|--------|--------|---------|-----------|----------|--------|----------|
|        |        |         |           |          | 1      | 2        |
| 3      | 4      | 5       | 6         | 7        | 8      | 9        |
| 10     | 11     | 12      | 13        | 14       | 15     | 16       |
| 17     | 18     | 19      | 20        | 21       | 22     | 23       |
| 24     | 25     | 26      | 27        | 28       | 29     | 30       |

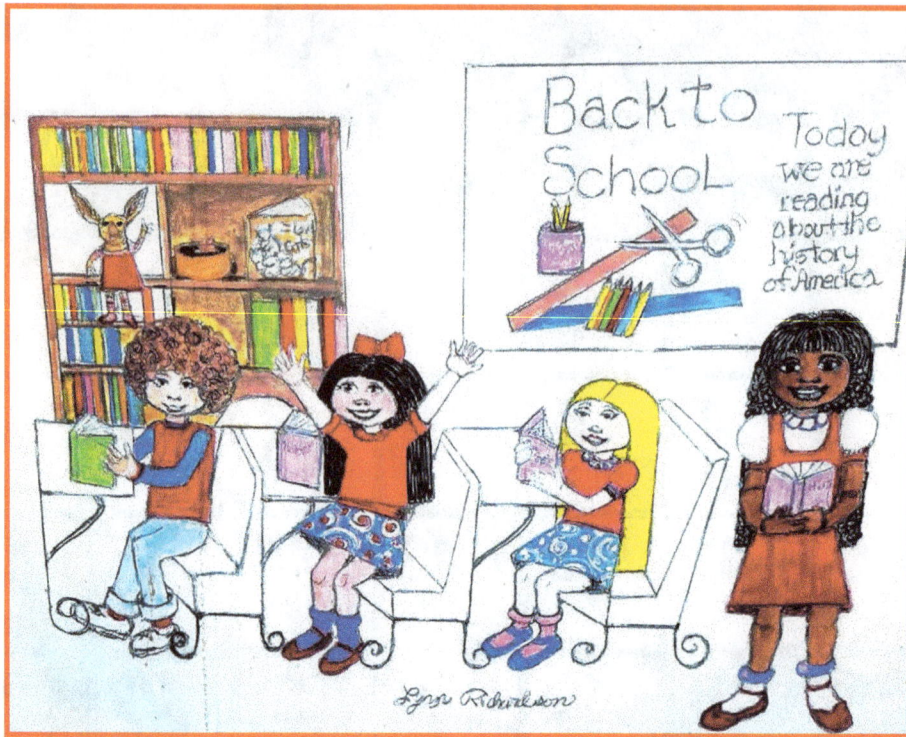

# SEPTEMBER

## EXPLORING COLONIAL AMERICA

https://www.PBSthirteen.org is a website that provides a variety of resources for bringing Colonial America to life in the classroom. The lesson plans in this website provide a series of media rich lessons designed for immediate use in the classroom. Students will be encouraged to explore what life was like in Colonial America. They can engage themselves in learning through popcorn readings and choral readings in books about colonial life and break up into discussion groups of four. Each group will do both oral and written presentations Their presentations will highlight what interested them the most about colonial life. Underneath students' written work will be some of their artwork which might include depictions of their family members being transported in time to Colonial settings. The artwork that will be displayed under the students' written work will reflect a colorful, creative, rich, assortment of students' pictures and paintings.

# SEPTEMBER

## A 2025 CALENDAR

| SUNDAY | MONDAY | TUESDAY | WEDNESDAY | THURSDAY | FRIDAY | SATURDAY |
|--------|--------|---------|-----------|----------|--------|----------|
|        | 1      | 2       | 3         | 4        | 5      | 6        |
| 7      | 8      | 9       | 10        | 11       | 12     | 13       |
| 14     | 15     | 16      | 17        | 18       | 19     | 20       |
| 21     | 22     | 23      | 24        | 25       | 26     | 27       |
| 28     | 29     | 30      | 31        |          |        |          |

# OCTOBER

## PUMPKINS, INDIANS, AND CORN HUSK DOLLS

http://www.teachersfirst.com is a website that teachers can use to share with their students on how to make Native American Indian corn husk dolls step by step. Students will work together in groups of four by concentrating on solving addition and subtraction problems through the use of employing plastic pumpkin counters or candy corn counters as math manipulative learning tools. Student groups can conduct research and engage in pair-share reading by reading and sharing stories about pumpkins, Indians, and corn.

# OCTOBER A 2025 CALENDAR

| SUNDAY | MONDAY | TUESDAY | WEDNESDAY | THURSDAY | FRIDAY | SATURDAY |
|--------|--------|---------|-----------|----------|--------|----------|
|        |        |         | 1         | 2        | 3      | 4        |
| 5      | 6      | 7       | 8         | 9        | 10     | 11       |
| 12     | 13     | 14      | 15        | 16       | 17     | 18       |
| 19     | 20     | 21      | 22        | 23       | 24     | 25       |
| 26     | 27     | 28      | 29        | 30       | 31     |          |

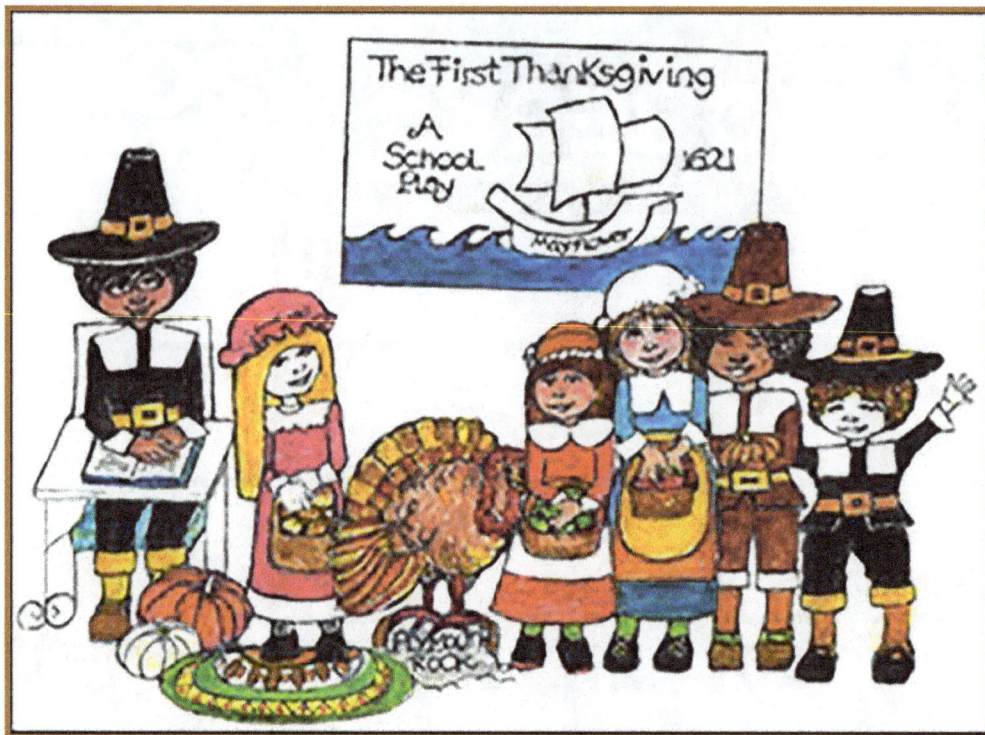

# NOVEMBER

## THE FIRST THANKSGIVING

https://www.education.world.com is a website that has a project entitled "Teach The Real Story of the First Thanksgiving" which includes an accurate telling of the first Thanksgiving starting with the reading of the Plymouth Thanksgiving story. https://www.education.world.com includes study and discussion questions with ideas for enrichment, art projects, and authentic recipes. Students will read stories about the first Thanksgiving. They can discover and explore how Squanto and other Native American Indian tribes helped show the Pilgrims how to plant corn. Squanto showed the Pilgrims how to survive in their newly discovered land. Students can engage in TPR activities (Total Physical Responses) by putting on their own versions in a re-enactment of the first Thanksgiving. Students need to explore the different points of views that should come out in these discussions. Students could have a roundtable discussion as they need to consider and write about the different viewpoints among the Pilgrims and the Indians.

# NOVEMBER

| SUNDAY | MONDAY | TUESDAY | WEDNESDAY | THURSDAY | FRIDAY | SATURDAY |
|--------|--------|---------|-----------|----------|--------|----------|
|  |  |  |  |  |  | 1 |
| 2 | 3 | 4 | 5 | 6 | 7 | 8 |
| 9 | 10 | 11 | 12 | 13 | 14 | 15 |
| 16 | 17 | 18 | 19 | 20 | 21 | 22 |
| 23 | 24 | 25 | 26 | 27 | 28 | 29 |
| 30 |  |  |  |  |  |  |

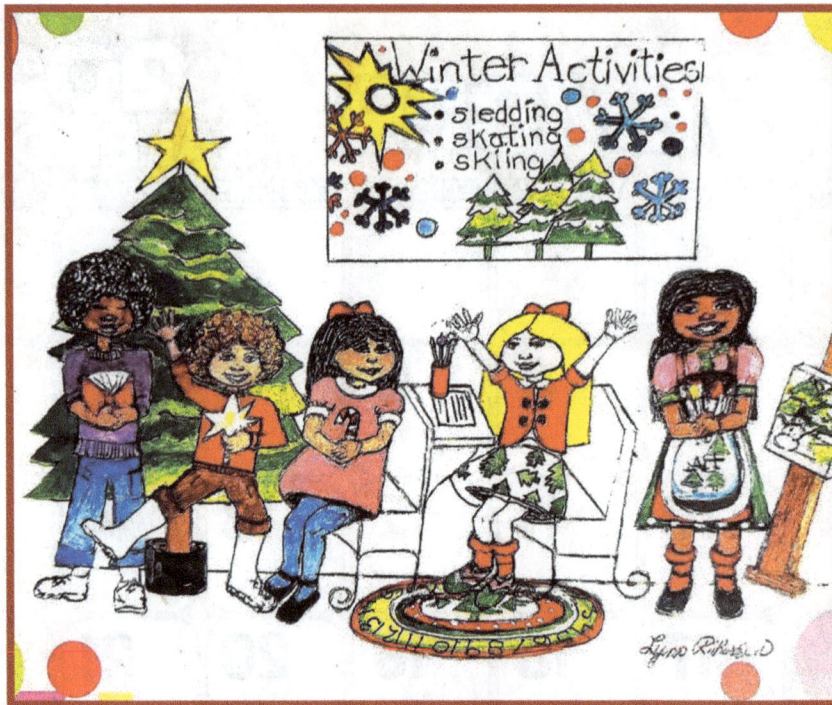

# DECEMBER

## HOLIDAYS & SNOWFLAKE DESIGNS

https://www.kids.nationalgeographic.com is a website where children can learn about unique tradition, celebrations, and holidays that occur around the world. https://www.education.world.com is a website in which children can capitalize student's excitement about December Holidays. The blog post titled "39 Fun ESL Games and Activities for an Exciting English Classroom" lists a variety of group activities that can be used to teach English in a fun and engaging way. The teacher will give out handouts on the winter season and snowflake formations.

Students can engage in research about how snowflakes are formed and will choose the snowflake formation they would like to design. After engaging in class discussions students will work with their teacher as the teacher passes out papers on how students can fold their snowflake design papers into various symmetrical and asymmetrical patterns and be able to cut out their designs. The students can paste them on to various shades of blue construction paper to display in the classroom as a small winter art display to celebrate the winter season.

# DECEMBER

## A 2025 CALENDAR

| SUNDAY | MONDAY | TUESDAY | WEDNESDAY | THURSDAY | FRIDAY | SATURDAY |
|--------|--------|---------|-----------|----------|--------|----------|
|        | 1 | 2 | 3 | 4 | 5 | 6 |
| 7 | 8 | 9 | 10 | 11 | 12 | 13 |
| 14 | 15 | 16 | 17 | 18 | 19 | 20 |
| 21 | 22 | 23 | 24 | 25 | 26 | 27 |
| 28 | 29 | 30 | 31 |   |   |   |

www.ingramcontent.com/pod-product-compliance
Lightning Source LLC
Chambersburg PA
CBHW080429030426
42335CB00020B/2657